HOW TO WIN THE
LOTTERY

*7 Secrets to Manifesting Your Millions
With the Law of Attraction*

© Copyright 2017 by Amy White - All rights reserved.

The following Book is reproduced below with the goal of providing information that is as accurate and as reliable as possible. Regardless, purchasing this Book can be seen as consent to the fact that both the publisher and the author of this book are in no way experts on the topics discussed within, and that any recommendations or suggestions made herein are for entertainment purposes only. Professionals should be consulted as needed before undertaking any of the action endorsed herein.

This declaration is deemed fair and valid by both the American Bar Association and the Committee of Publishers Association and is legally binding throughout the United States.

Furthermore, the transmission, duplication or reproduction of any of the following work, including precise information, will be considered an illegal act, irrespective whether it is done electronically or in print. The legality extends to creating a secondary or tertiary copy of the work or a recorded copy and is only allowed with express written consent of the Publisher. All additional rights are reserved.

The information in the following pages is broadly considered to be a truthful and accurate account of facts, and as such any inattention, use or misuse of the information in question by the reader will render any resulting actions solely under their purview. There are no scenarios in which the publisher or the original author of this work can be in any fashion deemed liable for any hardship or damages that may befall them after undertaking information described herein.

Additionally, the information found on the following pages is intended for informational purposes only and should thus be considered, universal. As befitting its nature, the information presented is without assurance regarding its continued validity or interim quality. Trademarks that mentioned are done without written consent and can in no way be considered an endorsement from the trademark holder.

Table of Contents

Introduction 1

Chapter 1: The Power of the Mind... 7

Chapter 2: The Law of Attraction... 13

Chapter 3: Optimizing Your Body, Mind, and Soul 23

Chapter 4: Manifesting Money Successfully 31

Chapter 5: Using Affirmations 39

Chapter 6: Using Creative Visualization................................ 47

Chapter 7: Recognizing opportunities and taking action . 57

Chapter 8: The missing ingredient – Appreciation 63

Chapter 9: Making the Law of Attraction Work for You...71

Chapter 10: Icing on the cake 79

Conclusion 89

Thank you!..93

INTRODUCTION

The mind is the key to creating reality. What you perceive in the physical world is rooted in your innermost thoughts and beliefs. If you want to attract what you plan to have and experience to become the master of your life, you should learn to control your thoughts.

Simply put, what happens in your life is a result of your thoughts and beliefs.

The state of your life, your finances, your relationships and your health is a reflection of your thoughts and your beliefs. Energy attracts energy.

According to Charles F. Haanel, *"thought power is the vibratory force formed by converting static mind into dynamic mind."* Your mind emits an invisible frequency that attracts a corresponding energy frequency.

This is the premise that the Law of Attraction is based on.

The Law of Attraction principle states that whatever is imaginable is achievable if you make a plan and act on it.

You can apply the Law of Attraction in all aspects of your life. You can obtain whatever you wish in life using the Law of Attraction.

Many things are possible using the power of your mind. It could be a healthy and toned body, your dream job, the right partner in life, financial success or even something as specific as winning the lottery.

Winning the lottery does not happen by pure luck. If you want to learn the secret, read this book and learn how.

This book will give you a step-by-step guide on how you can use the Law of Attraction to increase your chances of winning the lottery.

This book will also discuss some proven techniques by lottery winners on how the power of the mind can be a powerful tool in getting what you most desired.

Each Chapter of the book will discuss each technique, including tips and tricks used by successful lottery winners.

The book does not claim that it will give you guaranteed wins, but it will help you increase your chances of winning the lottery as proven in our sample success stories.

What are you waiting for? Start reading so you can get moving towards reaching that goal of winning the biggest lottery game of your life.

Your Free Gift

As a way of saying thanks for your purchase, I wanted to offer you a free bonus E-book called "*How to Talk to Anyone: 50 Best Tips and Tricks to Build Instant Rapport*" by my friend Ryan James.

Within this comprehensive guide, you will find information on:

- How to make a killer first impression

- Tips on becoming a great listener

- Using the FORM method for asking good questions

- Developing a great body language

- How to never run out of things to say

- Bonus chapters on Persuasion, Emotional Intelligence, and How to Analyze People

To grab your free bonus book just tap here, or go to:

http://ryanjames.successpublishing.club/freebonus/

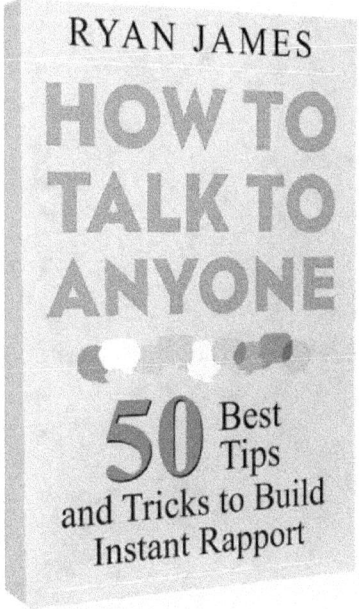

CHAPTER 1

THE POWER OF THE MIND

Quantum Physics described every object in the universe as frequencies of wavelengths and particles. Your thoughts are frequencies of wavelengths emitted and translated into the physical plane. You can achieve whatever your mind conceives.

You go through life without being conscious of your thoughts. When things happen, you put it down to fate or circumstances. The truth is, whatever happens to you is a result of your thought process.

Do you want proof?

Look at yourself. What are you now? A Mother? A Doctor? Perhaps a runway model? or a Writer? Try to remember yourself as a child. What did you dream of becoming someday? Maybe you dreamed of becoming the top runway model or a doctor. What things did you do to make those dreams come true? Did you ever think of yourself as a bum? Probably not or you would not be where you are right now.

What you have become is a result of how you thought from childhood to adulthood. Your thoughts dictated the things you needed to do to reach your dream. Your life is like a science experiment.

You dream that one day you will be a doctor. As you were growing up, the probabilities of fulfilling your dream will depend on how you act and how you think. In the process of trying to fulfill your dream, you experiment. You test ideas and situations to see if it would lead you to your goal.

If you want to change your life, change the way you think. Success comes to those who believe they can succeed and do something about it. If you want to achieve your goal, you have to change your way of thinking and beliefs.

If you want to win the lottery, think of yourself as a winner.

Change your life with the power of your mind

Your mind has two parts, your conscious mind, and your subconscious mind. Inside your conscious mind lies your subconscious mind. Your conscious mind acts as a filter while your subconscious mind is like a sponge that absorbs everything impressed on it by your conscious mind, be it negative or positive thoughts.

In an interview with Dr. Bruce H. Lipton, on the conscious and subconscious minds, he said that the subconscious is more powerful than the conscious mind. The conscious mind works only 5% of the time, and the subconscious mind takes over 95% of the time.

In Piaget's stages of cognitive development, from the sensorimotor stage to the preoperational stage a child learns through observation and using intuition. The child learns motor skills and sensory experiences by observing the world around him. The child's subconscious mind records all these observations and learning which would, later on, shape his character.

Your conscious mind can filter thoughts while your subconscious mind will process everything without a filter and if repeatedly ingrained would eventually become a habit. These habits are programs that direct your actions.

By the time you learned to allow your conscious thoughts to surface, your perception of the world, be it negative or positive becomes your truth. If your perception is negative, your subconscious mind will generate negative behaviors.

Tapping the shadows of your mind

Your conscious mind is your creative mind and thinking mind. Your conscious mind expresses your wants, needs, and desires but it will not tell you how to go about obtaining your desires. Your subconscious mind will dictate that. However, deeply rooted in your subconscious mind are your unused potentials blocked by the negative perceptions you acquired over the years of cognitive development. These blockages are like shadows that can affect your life.

The subconscious mind stores repressed emotions, hurts, disappointments, grief as well as dysfunctional beliefs that keep your undeveloped potentials to surface and allowing the possibility of self-transformation.

In Siddhartha Gautama Buddha's words, *"All that we are is the result of what we have thought. The mind is everything. What we think we become."*

In other words, your thoughts, beliefs, and attitude mirror your life. You are unconsciously creating your reality using the power of your mind. What happens in the physical world is a result of how you think and believe. Everything stored in your subconscious mind programmed you to perceive this to be the truth. These are your dominant thoughts.

Luckily, you can reprogram these programs. You can tap the shadows lurking behind your subconscious mind.

If you want to obtain this great power, you must teach yourself to control the nature of your dominant thoughts and realign yourself with the Universe. If you apply this, your life will transform in unimaginable ways.

Remember that your subconscious mind directs your actions. If you reprogram your subconscious mind to be more positive, it will generate a positive behavior and your actions will become positive.

You will reap what you sow, if you imprint positive thoughts and beliefs in your subconscious mind, it will attract things and circumstances aligned to your thoughts. You will gain what you desire most.

Such is the premise of the Law of Attraction.

CHAPTER 2

THE LAW OF ATTRACTION

The Law of Attraction

The Law of Attraction is the ability to attract to yourself anything that you focus on.

Based on the new thought philosophy, the Law of Attraction is the belief that what you think of is what you attract into your life.

According to the new thought philosophy, the mind and the body are vibrating energies. In Quantum Physics, we learned that the Universe is full of energy frequencies and therefore, we are made of energy.

The mind has two parts, the conscious or thinking mind and the subconscious or storage mind. Ideas and creativity come from the conscious mind. These ideas pass the conscious mind to the subconscious mind where it gets stored as information. The subconscious mind absorbs everything the conscious mind encounters.

During the cognitive development years, your mind absorbs everything you see around you. Every single event, word, thoughts, action, sound, and feeling passed from the conscious mind to the subconscious mind. The subconscious mind is like a storage tank that keeps everything stored inside. The information it stores is, later on, use as a response to any stimuli.

You know that your body is a mass of energy and your thoughts are energy, which means, that whatever you think of is made of energy. Therefore, if you think of positive thoughts, then your subconscious mind will also store positive thoughts. These positive thoughts give off a vibration of positive energy attracting a similar energy.

At this point, you are probably still not convinced so allow me to illustrate. As a child, you grew up believing that Santa Claus brings your gifts every Christmas. Our subconscious mind stored the information that every Christmas we find a gift under the Christmas tree that says it is from Santa. The program inside your subconscious mind is to believe that Christmas equates to a gift from Santa. Every year, you make a wish to Santa Claus so that he could bring your gift.

By now, you know it was not Santa putting those gifts under the tree but for a long time, you believed in Santa because inside your subconscious mind is the stored knowledge of the image and the story of Santa Claus. The program in your subconscious mind responds to the stimuli created by your conscious mind about Santa Claus by tapping in on its stored data.

Do you remember how you felt when you discovered the truth? Did it change your belief? Perhaps for some, yes, but for the majority the story remains real because until now, the tale of Santa Claus lives. That is how powerful the subconscious mind is. The subconscious mind can turn beliefs into what we perceive as truths.

Using the Law of Attraction

Now you know the power of your subconscious mind. How can you relate this to the principle of the Law of Attraction?

Your body is like a human magnet that sends out energy frequencies through your thoughts and emotions and in turn, these frequencies attract similar energy frequencies.

Have you ever experience losing a job opportunity because you failed in an interview? Have you ever thought why you failed? Go back to your subconscious mind. You go to an interview all prepped up and eager to go but once faced with the interviewer, self-doubts assail you. These doubts did not materialize in an instant. It was already there long before your interview.

Probably in the past, things happened that led you to believe you are not good enough. It happened often enough until it programs you to believe that this is the truth. A failing grade in school or someone bullied you in school could have caused you to believe that you are not worthy of anything.

In this scenario, you are allowing negative thoughts to enter your mind. These negative thoughts are triggering similar negative information in your subconscious mind. As a result, your subconscious mind will emit negative vibrations. These negative vibrations will translate into various forms like stuttering, nervous hand gestures or wobbly voice. These negative reactions will attract the same negative response, failing the interview.

Unknowingly, you are using the law of attraction to your disadvantage.

Using the Law of Attraction to your advantage

Your thoughts are the mirror images of your life. Fate or circumstances do not create your future, you do. Unfortunately, it is not easy to change the programs stored in your mind.

These limiting beliefs controlled what you can become by making a paradigm shift. Paradigms are the habits formed by the subconscious mind. These are the information rooted deep within your subconscious mind since birth.

If your paradigms are all negative, then you will only attract negative energy. Remember that the law of attraction attracts what you want to bring to yourself.

It has been a common belief that what you give out to the world will return to you tenfold. If you give to others, you will receive from others as well.

Using the Law of Attraction for Money

You can use the law of attraction for almost any of your desire be it health, love life, weight problems or money problems.

For many, the law of attraction is most commonly use to get abundant wealth.

Arguably, everyone wants money.

But why?

Good Vibe Coach, Jeannette Maw tells why. In her book '3 LOA Keys to unlock your Financial Fortune', she said that people want money because of what they think it can do for them.

She stated further, '*Money is the ultimate middleman. It was actually designed for that specific purpose – to make it easier for us to get what we want."*

Everyone dreams of living the good life, a big house, fast and expensive cars, designer label clothes, or a dream vacation. To have this, you need money and not just a few thousand dollars. You need lots of money.

It is not a sin to be rich. There is no law in the universe that says you cannot be rich. Everyone has an equal opportunity to become rich. It is how you think and act that will determine whether you will succeed or not.

You have to be ready to take a paradigm shift. You have to be ready to leave all your negative habits and reprogram your subconscious mind to accept new beliefs. It will not be comfortable because change has never been comfortable. You need to reprogram years of information that has already become your habits.

A paradigm shift is your first step towards making the law of attraction works for you.

The Law of Attraction Can Transform Your Life

Your life can transform dramatically by using the Law of Attraction to your advantage.

Here are a few things how mastering the law of attraction can enhance your life:

- You learn to trust your instincts and follow your intuition. You do not overthink and instead allow your emotions to direct you on the right path.

- You can increase the power of your dreams. As your thoughts grow larger and more powerful, you can dwell and believe more in your dreams. You can get more ideas on mapping out new paths towards fulfilling your goal.

- You can take control of your thoughts and shift your focus on more positive thoughts rather than the negative ones.

- You move one step closer to fulfill your dreams. Though success requires consistent work and action, it is empowering to know that every positive thought you have moves you closer to your goal.

- Your belief about success will change. If you think success is exclusive to a privileged few, the law of attraction will show you that it is possible for everyone to achieve success.

- You will become more productive and instead of wallowing on your mistakes, you give more focus on your goals and achieving them.

- You will have more control over your future and not at the mercy of others. Your positivity affects your interpersonal relationships by attracting better bonds.

Preparing yourself

In order to reprogram your subconscious mind, you need to prepare yourself. You are going to battle with years of old habits deeply rooted in your subconscious mind.

You need to get ready in body, mind and soul.

CHAPTER 3

OPTIMIZING YOUR BODY, MIND, AND SOUL

Overcoming years of habit is not easy. These habits programmed your mind with negativity and reprogramming your mind is going to be an uphill battle.

You cannot simply erase years of habit in just one click or reprogram your mind to do something different. Your brain, your body, and your soul should be in tune.

Negative thoughts can drain the energy from your body, leaving you tired and unable to have the strength to stick to your goals.

A regular positive routine can give you structure and the strength to handle yourself when things get rough.

Positive routines will help you set your priorities, avoid procrastination and help you keep track of your goal. You need these elements to apply the law of attraction to yourself.

Optimizing your Body

Your body is the temple of your mind and soul. You need to keep your body strong and healthy to keep your mind and spirit healthy.

If your body is not functioning well, it affects your brain activity and spiritual balance. If you are sick, you cannot think right or make a plan.

Have you ever felt good even with a raging headache?

To keep your body healthy and strong, you have to take care of it properly. Here are few tips on how you can optimize your body.

- Eat foods that can help stimulate your brain. The food you eat affects your brain functions. Select the food groups that can help your brain operate optimally. When your brain is optimized, it sends out a message to your body to let it know that all is well. Food groups that can help optimize your brain include:

- *Fish.* Fish is the classic brain food. Fish is rich in oil and fortified with omega 3 and fatty acids that are essential in the brain function and development. Omega 3 is also good for the heart as it reduces stroke. It is also a good memory enhancer.

- *Nuts and Seeds.* Nuts and seeds contain antioxidants and Vitamin E that help prevent cognitive decline.

- *Chocolates, particularly dark chocolates.* Unbelievably, chocolate can be healthy in moderation. Dark chocolates contain antioxidants that slow down cognitive decline and caffeine, which are a natural stimulant and a concentration booster.

- Other food groups include fruits such as avocado, blueberries and carrots.

- Drink Water or Tea. Drink plenty of water, about 9-13 cups a day. Do not allow yourself to become dehydrated. Drink a glass of water in the morning and make sure you drink after each meal. If you have had enough water, alternate it with tea. Some tea variety can help fight against illness.

  o Green tea has anti-cancer effects and good for the circulatory system and the brain.

  o White tea can help prevent cancer.

  o Black tea is good for the lungs.

  o Oolong tea can help lower bad cholesterol.

- Do physical exercises. Do not be a couch potato. The best way to keep your body healthy is through exercising. Most people hate doing exercises. You do not have to do backbreaking and grueling exercises. There are fun exercises like dancing, Zumba, aerobics, stretching and even as simple as walking down the grocery store. The point here is to get your body moving.

- Do breathing exercises. Practice deep breathing. Your lungs release toxins by exhaling.

- Get enough sleep. Lack of sleep can affect your overall mood, judgment, and ability to retain information. Lack of sleep can affect your brain and could lead to diseases like diabetes and cardiovascular diseases.

Optimizing your mind

When your body is healthy, your mind follows. A healthy mind can give you a positive outlook. You can further optimize your mind with the following simple tips:

- Start your day on a positive note. Do not think of anything negative. Use a mantra if necessary and keep saying it aloud so when the day starts to get tough, recite your mantra. Maintain a positive outlook even under those worst circumstances. Remember, what make things good or bad is not the circumstances surrounding it, but rather how you respond to it. Do not allow the negativity to overcome you easily.

- Be proactive and not reactive. Do not wait for things to happen and instead make things happen by acting on it. Focus on your task and do what needs to be done to move forward.

- Visualize your success. Author Jack Canfield of 'Chicken Soup for the Soul' book series said, practicing visualization ten minutes a day could harness the power of your subconscious mind. The imagination can work wonders. Just imagine yourself listening to the announcement that your lottery ticket is the winning number.

- Taking Regular Breaks the entire day. Doing all these tips can become overwhelming at best so giving your mind a break is acceptable. Though designed to help you, it should not take over your life completely. Taking a break helps to keep your focus and break the monotony of your exercises.

Optimizing your Soul

Tending to your body also requires tending to yourself spiritually. Cleanse your spirit to remove the bad vibes. Get your spirit in tune with your mind. When these two are in tune, they make a powerful combination.

Here are few suggested ways to help optimize your spirit.

- Do meditation. Meditation is a technique used to rest your mind. In a state of meditation, your mind is cleared and inwardly focused. You are fully awake, yet your conscious mind is unaware of the external events happening around you. Meditation can help you to:

    o Decrease feelings of depression and irritability.

    o Decrease muscle tension, stress and pain.

    o Improve your brain's ability to control your thoughts and reactions.

- Practice Gratitude. Learn to appreciate the things you have and be thankful for them.

Practicing gratitude teaches you that not everything turns out the way you want it to but you are still thankful for the things that come your way. Further, the more gratitude you give out, the more blessings you attract.

- Learn to give to others. As the saying goes, "it is better to give than to receive." Giving to others gives you a certain feeling of satisfaction that no amount of material thing could equal. It does not have to be material.

Simple things like carrying the bag of grocery for your neighbor, or complimenting a co-worker on her new haircut makes a big impact on both your day. Seeing the smile of happiness on someone's face and knowing that you are responsible for it leaves an uplifting feeling to your heart.

CHAPTER 4

MANIFESTING MONEY SUCCESSFULLY

At this point, you already have a good idea behind the principle of the law of attraction.

You might ask, so what is next?

The next step is manifesting what you want.

Your next question would probably be, what is manifestation? Is it the same as the law of attraction?

The answer is no. The law of attraction is the result of manifestation.

So what is manifestation?

Manifestation is bringing into focus all the ingredients you need to get you to your goal. Manifestation is the bridge towards achieving your one true desire.

When everything starts to align, it means the law of attraction is working.

The Big Mistake

Many people think the law of attraction is like a magic wand. You whip it up and out comes your wish.

This is the reason why many of those who tried using the law of attraction failed. Nothing ever comes instantly. Persistence is the key.

You have to be firm in your resolve and your belief that what you want is attainable. If things do not come out the way you want it to, do not abandon it. Try to persevere and try again.

Most people have very little patience and endurance. They often jump from one thing to another because they do not have the perseverance to wait.

The law of attraction will come to you when it feels that the time is right. Things will happen at the right time and not when you command it to happen.

Effective ways to guarantee your manifestation success

Many people still find it difficult to master the law of attraction. The problem is people think that the law of attraction is simply to make a goal and wait for the Universe to hand it to them on a silver platter.

If you want something, you have to do some work in order to attain it. Here are a few things that you can do to guarantee manifestation success:

Be specific with what you want

There are probably a million and one things that you want to have in life. However, are they really the things that you need or you just want it because it is nice to have? You need to be specific about what you want.

You have to look deep within yourself and find out your innermost wish or desire. Do not wish for the moon but instead, wish to visit the moon. In short, do not wish for the impossible and for things you do not really need.

If you want abundance in life, be specific. Is it money, a house, a car, or a business? What is your reason for wanting it? You have to be clear so that the vibrations you send out will attract the same vibrations from the universe.

If your mind gets flooded with so many things, write it down. Make a list of the things you want and then review them. Find out which ones are the things you want but you can do without. This will help narrow down your list.

Be firm and act with conviction

One of the pitfalls of the law of attraction is the lack of conviction. Most of the time, you work on what you want but your heart is not really on it. You wish for it but deep inside, you do not really believe that you can get it.

As a result, when things do not work out the way you expect it to, you walk away and give up or you change your goal and start a new one. The cycle becomes repetitive because every time you do not get the desired result.

Why is this happening?

You are following every rule and step in the law of attraction. Why is it not working?

The truth is it is working. The problem is it is working against you. Your doubts and insecurities are rooted deep inside you. Although you keep practicing the principles of the law of attraction, you do not really believe that it is attainable.

Your mind absorbed many negative thoughts, which are now deeply rooted in your subconscious mind. These thoughts are negative frequencies that your mind emits to the Universe.

Like frequencies attract the same like frequencies, this is the foundation of the principle of the law of attraction. If you harbor negativity, no matter how you tried you will never get the result that you are aiming for.

As a result, you end up jumping from one thing to another. You never finish anything because the moment you get frustrated over something, you abandon it and start on something else.

When you want to manifest something, you have to be firm with your resolve. You need to make sure of what you want and that you would stick to it regardless of the outcome.

Once your resolve is firm and unshakeable, you have to strengthen it with conviction. Trust and believe that the Universe will give you what you want. Do not waver in that belief despite the odds.

Failure is not inevitable

The most destructive negative thought that you can ever have is the belief that failure is inevitable.

That is not true. It is not what you do that makes failure inevitable. It is what you think and believes that makes failure inevitable.

If you believe that you will fail, then everything you do will result in failure. Keep in mind that like frequencies attract like frequencies. If you allow your negative beliefs to rule your life, you will get nowhere.

If you believe that you will fail, then everything you do will result in failure. The universe will give whatever your mind conceives.

Until you free yourself from these negative beliefs, you will only attract negative results.

Make a Paradigm Shift

You grew up believing that everything you know, feel, see and hear is the absolute truth so when your brain tells you to act on this belief, you follow suit.

Many times, you hear the sound of your thoughts speaking to you, dictating your every move. You believe that it is you thinking those thoughts out but the truth is that these are just images and visions embedded in your subconscious mind.

Change your belief by making a paradigm shift.

Erase your negative thoughts and replace them with positive ones. It may sound easier said than done. Changing a habit and belief of a lifetime is not easy.

The mind can be a powerful foe or ally. Instinct protects us from anything foreign and the mind controls the instinct.

However, it is not impossible. You can find a thousand and one tips in books and articles about how to make a paradigm shift but until you allow your conscious mind to take over your subconscious mind, it will not be possible.

Icing on the cake

You will find that in other books about the law of attraction, there are other elements to a successful manifestation like visualization, affirmation, and being grateful.

These are just icing on the cake. These elements strengthen the other four elements mentioned above.

No amount of visualization or affirmation will work if you failed to do the four basic elements to a successful manifestation.

Once you have mastered the first four, support it with visualization tools and affirmations.

CHAPTER 5

USING AFFIRMATIONS

One of the ingredients of a successful manifestation is an affirmation.

Manifestation is similar to cooking a dish. You need to prepare the ingredients and spices to make a delicious and mouth-watering dish.

A dish will taste different if an ingredient is missing. It is the same with manifestation. You can list as many intentions as you want but if there is a missing ingredient, you will have a half-cooked result.

To make the law of attraction works for you, you have to take action by doing exercises that will strengthen it. One of those is exercising affirmations.

Many people who wish to manifest something use affirmations to strengthen their wish.

What is an affirmation?

Affirmations are positive words that you speak or listen to repeatedly, to strengthen and align your emotions and vibrations to your intention.

In the early stage of a person's development, repetition is the easiest way for the brain to retain information.

If you lived your life in negativity, this is rooted in your mind so whenever you try to manifest something, you always fail because of the limiting beliefs you have.

The key to using affirmation is repetition, but it has to be a positive affirmation. Here are a few easy ways to a successful affirmation:

1. Make your affirmation related to your intention. You cannot make an affirmation about something that you do not want. It has to relate with your wish or intent.

Example: *If you wish for abundance, make your affirmation related to wealth and abundance. "I am a millionaire. I have abundance in wealth."*

2. Write a list of your affirmations in the present tense. When you write your affirmations, always write it as if you have already achieved it. It should be in a first-person statement.

   Example: *"I am rich. I have all the money I need."*

3. Your affirmations should always be positive. Do not entertain negative thoughts. Believe in your affirmations and let the positivity washed over you.

   Example: *"This number won me the lottery."*

4. Recite your affirmations often. Repetition will ingrain them to your subconscious mind until it becomes a reality. Make your affirmation sound like an incantation until it becomes deeply rooted in your subconscious mind.

   Example: *You can record your affirmation and play the recording over and over again.*

Eliminate Negative thoughts

Affirmation should always be positive. Do not entertain negative thoughts. Positive affirmation helps you manifest successfully.

You can combat negative thoughts by following these five simple techniques:

1. *Bar it.* When negative thoughts enter your mind, stop it. Bar it from infiltrating your thoughts. Replace the thought with something positive. Most people by nature are pessimistic. Negative thoughts are second nature to them. If you recognize a sign that a negative thought is about to enter your mind, cut it off and think of something else.

2. *Put a name to it.* Since negative thoughts are second nature to some people, the barring technique will not work. Another technique they can do is labeling. Put a name to it so you can belittle it. Tell yourself it is merely a negative thought. Do not allow it to overtake you. Keep repeating those words to yourself until the thought becomes meaningless. Do not give it power by reacting to it.

3. ***Make it less powerful.*** Turn your negative thoughts into something silly and funny to rob its power. Exaggerate it to the point where it would look ridiculous even to think about it. Without power, it cannot affect you.

4. ***Go the other way.*** When a negative thought creeps up to you, go the other way. Counteract it with an opposite thought. The mind can only think one thought at a time. It may seem that a million thoughts are in your mind but in reality, you are thinking them one at a time at a faster pace so it would seem that you are thinking multiple thoughts at the same time. So if something negative starts to enter your mind, immediately think of a positive thought to crush its power.

5. ***Embed positive thoughts.*** Recite your positive thoughts aloud and repeat it continuously until all thoughts of negativity are gone. The technique uses an affirmation that we will discuss in detail in the next Chapter.

You can use any of these five techniques or a combination of them. The important thing to remember is that affirmation will be useless if you are entertaining negative thoughts.

Making your affirmations powerful

Your affirmation should always start with the word "I" as if you are already claiming the success of your intent.

It should always be positive.

Here are some helpful tips on how to make your affirmations more powerful.

- It has to be believable to you. There is no point in writing affirmations that you yourself doubt. This will only create negativity thus preventing your intent from manifesting.

- Include the word "thank you" in your affirmations. This will make your affirmation sound as if you already achieved success

- Recite your affirmations first thing in the morning when you wake up and the last thing in the evening before you sleep.

- Include your affirmations during meditations. Meditations put your mind in a relaxed state.

- Make your affirmations visible. Write them on sticky notes, or on a whiteboard, or you can use it as a screen saver for your laptop. Place it anywhere within your line of vision.

CHAPTER 6

USING CREATIVE VISUALIZATION

Creative visualization is another main ingredient of a successful manifestation.

Visual tools can help attain a successful manifestation but for many, it turned to frustration. No matter how they do the visualization exercise, it does not seem to work.

Making an effective visualization

Visualization is the state where you imagine yourself basking in the manifestation of your intention.

Here are some techniques for a more effective visualization exercise.

- Do not just imagine it, feel it happening. When you visualize, do not just imagine that your intention has manifested. Try to imagine the actual feeling of enjoying your success.

Visualize this:

Imagine opening the doors of your brand new house. Imagine yourself walking inside the house. As you stepped inside the house, imagine the feeling of euphoria you feel owning your dream house. Feel the happiness at that exact moment as you imagine yourself holding the keys to your brand new house.

- There is always a positive aspect. When a negative thought comes to mind, do not fight it. Allow it to flow then slowly tell yourself in every bad thing that happens, there is always a positive aspect.

Visualize this:

Using the new house scenario, you feel good about finally realizing that dream. Then a negative thought pops up. There is a fire destroying your house. Do not fight it. The more you fight the negative thought, the more it persists. Instead, think of something positive.

The firefighters arriving in time to save your burning house. The damage is minimal and repair is possible.

- See it as if you are living it. Do not imagine it as if you are watching it from happening. Live in it, as if you are there at that exact moment.

Visualize this:

Instead of imagining your house and seeing what it looks like, imagine yourself living in that house. Imagine touching every nook and cranny of that house. You feel the coldness of the brick stones as you ran your palm against the walls.

- Believe that your intention has manifested. Do not think of your intention in the future tense. Think of it in the present tense as if it is already there. It is a done deal and you do not have to do anything else for it to manifest.

Visualize this:

Imagine that you already have your dream house. Imagine that you are already living in that house. You are not dreaming about your house because it is already there. There is nothing else to do but smile at your good fortune.

Visualization Tools

You can use visual tools to enhance your visualization exercise. You can choose to use all or some of these tools.

The important thing to remember when using visual tools is that these are merely representations related to what you want.

Here are some inspiring techniques on creating your visual tools:

Creating a dream board

A dream board is an inexpensive tool that you can use in your visualization exercise. You can create it using scrap materials and any natural objects lying around the house.

Using the dream house scenario, you can try creating this sample visual tool.

Materials:

Cork board or you can use an old wood panel to use as your baseboard

Cut out pictures of money, the more money cutouts you have the better

A picture of your dream house

You can include pictures that you can use as representations of wealth and abundance.

Preparation:

- Use the baseboard to pin the cutouts you have.

- Put the picture of your dream house in the center and surround it with money cutouts (you can also draw the images of money if you cannot find cutouts).

- On the four corners, you can put the other representations of wealth or add some of your affirmations.

- Display the board in a place where you can see it often. You can create as many boards as you like and put it around your house.

- Now you have your dream board.

Visual affirmations

Your affirmations are also visual tools that you can use in your visualization exercise. You can make creative affirmations by doing the following suggestions:

- You can write your affirmations on colored papers and use them as signboards. Place them in areas relating to your goal like your dream board.

- Place them on your smartphones. You can set it as an alarm or as a lock screen visual or as the wallpaper on your smartphone.

- You can create dream journals. You can write down your affirmations on a diary or a journal specifically created for that purpose. Write on it daily. You can include how you want to design your dream house. Remember, the key to a successful affirmation is repetition.

Mental Visualization

Mental visualization is creating or building images of your intention using the mind. Instead of physical images, you use your mind to build them.

A great way to do mental visualization is through meditation.

Visualize this sample exercise:

Find a comfortable spot and get yourself in a meditative state. Relax and free your mind of negativity. Think of an image that represents your intent. It could be the lottery ticket or your lottery number combination. It could be an image of money or a brand new house and car. Use any image you want that you could associate with your intent.

Play with different images until you find the one that speaks to you. The image should give you the feeling of success. Focus on that image and hold in your mind for 10 minutes.

You can do this repeatedly throughout the day. Use the same image in your succeeding mental visualization.

Verbal visualization

Verbal visualization is like verbal affirmation but you add a story script using "as if" scenarios.

You recite your affirmations and role-play verbally the "as if" scenarios. Your imagination plays a vital role in verbal visualizations.

Here is a sample exercise using the dream house scenario:

Imagine that you already have your dream house. If you already have a location for your dream house, you can go there or if not, imagine your present house as if it is your dream house.

Go to your lawn or your garage and pretend you are seeing a wide-open space.

"I will buy a new house with a garage to fit my 5 cars. Here, I will place my Peugeot and next to it my Porsche. My infinity pool will be in this corner, and right beside it is a Jacuzzi and sauna. "

Go back inside your house and continue affirming verbally.

"This is my son's bedroom. The space on the left will be his bed, on the right his drum set so he could practice. The room is soundproof to keep the noise. That door on the other side is my daughter's bedroom. Inside the bedroom is her dollhouse so it would be easier for her to play with her dolls. The master's bedroom is the grandest room."

This is living "as if" you already won the lottery. Remember your thoughts create your reality.

CHAPTER 7

RECOGNIZING OPPORTUNITIES AND TAKING ACTION

One of the pitfalls that many fall into when using the law of attraction is that they tend to focus on the outcome.

The outcome becomes so important that many fail to notice the opportunities coming their way, opportunities that will bring them closer to reaching their goal.

Common Pitfalls why you lose opportunities

When you focus on the outcome, you become more selective of the opportunities coming in your way.

Your greatest enemy is yourself. You lose these opportunities because you allow fear and self-doubt to rule you.

Here are some tips that you can avoid in order not to miss the next opportunity:

- Wallowing in your past mistake. If you missed an opportunity the first time, do not miss it a second time. Do not wallow in your past mistake. If you missed it, forget about it. Do not wallow in self-regret or beat yourself up for missing an opportunity. Move on and watch out for the next opportunity.

- Fear of the competition. Do not fear competition and instead trust in your ability to win. If an opportunity presents itself, do not hesitate to grab it. Trust your passion for your work to help you win against the competition.

- Believing that fate is working against you. The Universe will give you everything you asked. The Universe is not selective. Whether what you want is good or bad if you asked for it, the Universe will grant it.

Recognizing the Signs

Admittedly, there are times when it is difficult to recognize if the signs you are receiving is really coming from the Universe or just your ego talking.

How can you tell the difference? Here are a few tips that the signs are coming from the Universe.

- You feel good about your actions. You know that your actions are not out of fear.

- Your action is spontaneous. You know that you are not directing the outcome of your action.

- The Universe sends signs unexpectedly and not because of manipulation or deliberately directing how things should happen.

The Universe can be bold and subtle. The signs you will receive may not always be obvious but you must learn to recognize them.

Learn to question the things that happen in your life. You can easily recognize the signs that the Universe is telling you something. The sign is usually out of the ordinary. It will be unexpected and subtle.

If these things happen, ask yourself why. Why did it turn out this way?

A lottery winner once said that before he won the lottery he would always feel the urge to pass by the lottery stand. He said that for several months now, he was thinking how nice it will be if he wins the lottery. He started buying lottery tickets in the hope of winning but after several weeks, he has yet to win a dime. He would often tell himself that he will win and that one of these days, he will win the lottery.

A week prior to winning, he felt the urge to buy a ticket from a seller near his office. He has been buying from the one near his home, which is more convenient but he felt this need to pass by the lottery seller near his office.

Finally, after three days of ignoring his feelings, he finally followed his urge and pass by the ticketing store near his office. After buying the ticket, he still bought another ticket from his old seller.

To his shock, the ticket he bought from the one near his office won the jackpot prize for that draw.

If he had ignored his instinct, he never would have won.

Taking Action

When an opportunity comes knocking, do not ignore it. Grab it and act on it.

As you apply the law of attraction, thoughts, events, and ideas related to your goal will come to you. Some will come in small portions while others will be grand. Act on everything that comes your way, big or small.

Often, small things are pathways that would lead you to bigger things and eventually towards attaining your goal.

You can make your goal but you do not just wait on it. You have to be responsible for it by taking action.

Trust your intuition

Keep an open mind and be sensitive to signs that what you manifested is near fruition. Here are some indicators that your intent is near its manifestation:

- *Seeing and hearing about what you want often.* When you are close to success, you notice of seeing signs that represent what you desire. If you manifested money, you could pick up a coin while walking down the street or often hear stories of winning the lottery from people around you.

- *You get small victories.* Often, the small things you tried manifesting comes to you easily. This is a sign that your biggest desire is possible. Grocery discount coupons, getting small refunds, these are small things related to your big manifestation of abundance wealth.

- *Your intuition gets sharper.* You just know and feel that your biggest desire is about to happen. Trust your intuition.

- *You feel more positive and happy.* You have eliminated the negativity and aligned your life with the Universe. The more aligned your life with the Universe the happier you feel. If this is possible, then you know that what you want is possible.

- *Roadblocks appear.* When roadblocks appear, do not worry about it. This is the Universe's way of asking if this is truly what you want. These roadblocks help strengthen you.

CHAPTER 8

THE MISSING INGREDIENT – APPRECIATION

The most overlooked ingredient to having a successful manifestation is gratitude and appreciation.

Gratitude and appreciation is just a tiny slice of the whole pie but its impact on the law of attraction is immense.

Take your list of intent for example. Go through and read each one carefully. Do you notice anything?

Take your wish for a high paying job. You are asking the Universe to help you attract a better job prospect but have you thanked the Universe for the current job you have? Granted, that this job sucks and you want something better but compared to a jobless person, your current situation is a heaven sent.

You complain how your present job sucks and that you can do better but to a jobless person, any job, as long as it pays is already a gift from the Universe. What about you? Have you thanked the Universe for having a job?

In a nutshell, if you do not know the good things you have at present and learn to appreciate them, it will be difficult for you to recognize the signs the Universe is giving you.

Start appreciating the good things in your life.

Learn to appreciate the things that you already have. It could be as simple as having a good job or getting a discount from the grocery.

As described by Eckhart Tolle, *"It is through gratitude for the present moment that the spiritual dimension of life opens up."*

Your desire for many things often blinds you to the things you already have. When you are aware of your blessings, and you give thanks for everything you have no matter how big or small, you attract more blessings into your life.

Showing your gratitude need not be extravagant or grand. Here are the top five ways that you can show gratitude:

1. *Express your gratitude.* Do not suppress your natural inclination to express your gratitude physically or verbally. Always give thanks for the help of others. Give your loved ones a hug even for just being there beside you. Including the word "thank you" can make a big difference.

2. *Show gratitude through appreciation.* Do not forget to look around you. Smell the flowers when you walk. No matter how stressed or busy you are, do not be blind to the beauty and goodness around you. Embrace the true meaning of appreciation, which is, to recognize and enjoy the qualities of something or someone. Show appreciation to the people around you.

3. *Show gratitude by giving back.* You can show gratitude by giving to others by giving back to

those who are in need. It need not be monetary. You can give your time, your assistance and your kindness. You can also show gratitude to yourself by taking care of your body and mind, and by loving yourself. Loving yourself is important because you are showing the Universe that you appreciate you.

4. *Show gratitude by listening.* Remember, the best friend to have is someone who not only gives good advice but someone who listens. Give your full attention to others when they are conversing with you. Do not let other things distract you. Show value to another person by listening to what he/she has to say without interruption or distraction. Listening can also be advantageous because you can hear opportunities knocking on your door.

5. *Show gratitude through acceptance.* Learn to accept and understand whatever circumstances come your way. Life is like a rollercoaster, you are up one moment and down the next minute. Do not be resistant to challenge,

accept and embrace it wholeheartedly. Challenges are the Universe's way to make you to take action.

Why gratitude is important

Gratitude is the best way to make your blessings count. It can help align your life positively. When using the law of attraction you often neglect giving gratitude, so here is a refresher on the basic laws of gratitude:

- The more you thank the Universe, the more opportunities will come your way.

- Giving thanks will make you happy. Be grateful for what you have and wait patiently for the things to come.

- Give thanks for whatever you have. When things are at its worst, find a positive aspect.

- Gratitude brings true forgiveness.

- Grateful mind do not take things for granted.

- Gratitude is not just saying it but living it.

- Gratitude means giving back.

Trust and Believe

This is the best time to let go and trust the Universe. Do not get obsessed with your desire. Ask yourself if you really need to win the lottery or you just want to win the lottery to buy the things you want.

Let it go and trust that the Universe will give you what you want. Get attached and detached from your dream at the same time. This way you are showing trust in the Universe by waiting for your dream to manifest in a relaxed and positive manner.

Living in the knowing

In this exercise, live in the knowledge that you already won the lottery jackpot. Describe how and where you will spend the money. Express gratitude in advance. You can do this through more verbal affirmations.

"I can buy that 7-bedroom house that I have been eyeing for some time. My kids will transfer to a private school. It feels good to have all this money to spend."

You can also express gratitude in advance or thank the Universe for every blessing you currently have.

"Thank you for a wonderful and patient family. Thank you for the money I won. I can now give them everything they need."

CHAPTER 9

MAKING THE LAW OF ATTRACTION WORK FOR YOU

You have taken every necessary step to make to manifest your dream by using the law of attraction and yet nothing seems to be happening.

Do not panic. Everything has its own time and it is possible that you still harbor lingering doubts as to the effectivity of the principle.

To Sum it up

As Thomas Troward said, *"The action of Mind plants that nucleus which, if allowed to grow undisturbed, will eventually attract to itself all the conditions necessary for its manifestation in outward visible form."*

In simple words, "ask, believe and receive", that is the law of attraction.

Ask

Set your goal. Do not be afraid to dream and dream big. One the most belittling thought that most people have is that dreams are only for the lucky ones. Money attracts money so only the rich will become richer.

When you set your goal, make sure that it is something that you really want. Be specific about your goal. Dream like a child.

Remember the time when you were a child and believe you can do anything and have everything. As you grow older, you lose your ability to be child-like. You allow negative thoughts to control you.

Use your dream board. Meditate to unlock and increase the power of your mind. Stay focus. If you want to be wealthy, be specific. How do you want to get that wealth? How much wealth do you need? Why do you need it? These are questions that you would need to answer, questions that would show you of what you truly desire.

Believe

Believe in the Universe. Trust its plan for you. Sometimes things happen that set you on a different path. Push your fear down and embrace it. There is always a reason for everything.

Do not allow the negativity around you to affect your belief. This is your dream, not theirs. Your thoughts and dreams are also the thoughts and dreams of the Universe.

Do not follow what others say and continue to trust in your thoughts. Just because others failed, it does not mean you would too.

Receive

Thank the Universe for everything you have, big or small. Gratitude is a powerful magnet for success.

Some tips on how you can increase gratitude:

- Develop a sense of awareness. Appreciate the beauty around you.
- Meditate to create a feeling of anticipation about the coming day.

- Write down your encounters with things you are thankful for.

- Remind yourself not to worry. Do not stress yourself out over negativity.

- Be kind for it breeds compassion giving way to more goodwill.

- Be happy.

- Thank people no matter how small the kindness they give you.

- Be thankful for what you have. Celebrate abundance and more will follow.

- Be thankful for your health.

- Reflect on your day and let the gratitude of having that day replenish you.

The more gratitude fills your heart, the more the Universe will respond by presenting you with more experiences that you can be thankful for.

Take action. Grab at every opportunity presented to you. Manifestation is not possible if you will not take any action.

Do not miss the signs that the Universe is sending you. If you manifested wealth, then be aware of the telltale signs that money is coming your way.

- You often encounter the number 8 in your activities. The number 8 is a lucky number to the Chinese people and supposedly brings good fortune.

- Ancient Chinese folklore believes that a new baby is equaled to good fortune. If you get pregnant, then good fortune is coming your way.

- Bugs visit your house. Another belief is that when insects and bugs visit your house, it symbolizes the arrival of good fortune.

- According to Feng Shui, keeping coins in your kitchen will help make you become more abundant.

There a lot of folklores and beliefs that you can use to tell if money is coming your way. You can choose to believe them or not. The important thing to remember is to take advantage of every opportunity presented your way.

If you need help, do not be afraid to ask. The Universe will at times give you things in disguise and if you are not sure what to do, then ask. Ask experts who can give you guidance and advice. Ultimately, you will make your own decision.

Winning the lottery using the law of attraction

Make it work by not caring about the money.

That may sound crazy but it is the truth. You manifested winning the lottery jackpot but do not let it run your life.

Remember the basic principle of the law of attraction, "you attract the same vibrations that you emit."

If you are so desperate to win, then the vibration you will emit is also that desperate need. Desperation is negative so it will only attract the same vibration of negativity.

Do not let your desire for money control how you feel and how you think. Do not let it stand in your way to achieve your dreams.

Yes, money is nice to have. It can buy you many materials things that could make you happy. But money is not the only thing that could make you happy.

Once you realize that money is not going to be the root of your happiness, you take the pressure off from the Universe from making it happen.

The more you want for money, the more elusive it becomes.

Get yourself to set off the right vibration and everything will fall into place.

Align your thoughts and trust the Universe to do the rest. If the Universe presents you with an opportunity, do not question it. Just take advantage of whatever comes your way.

Do whatever makes you feel good and trust the Universe will not send you something that you will not like or enjoy.

Always remember, when you ask, you have to believe before you can receive.

CHAPTER 10

ICING ON THE CAKE

Attaining a successful manifestation is like baking a cake.

You have to have the right ingredients, and the measurement should be exact and precise.

The cake will not bake itself, you need to mix the ingredients and bake it in the oven. The same with manifestation, you cannot have a successful manifestation if you do not have the elements to apply the law of attraction and act on it.

With all these said, you can begin applying the law of attraction now.

How to make a successful Manifestation - Confession of a Lottery Jackpot Winner

You probably heard stories of many lottery jackpot winners sharing their stories of how they won the lottery using the law of attraction.

This story is about Joe (not his real name) who shared his story on how he attained a successful manifestation.

Joe is not new to the principle of the law of attraction. He already heard a lot of law of attraction coaches saying that winning the lottery is possible using the law of attraction.

Although he has his misgivings, Joe learned more about the law of attraction and started applying it in his life. Below are the steps that Joe took to attain a manifestation miracle.

- Clarity of intention. Be clear with what you want. Make sure that it is something that you really want in your life and not just something nice to have.

Joe's story:

There are so many things that Joe wants in his life. Joe has a wife and two kids and earning a decent wage.

However, he wants more. He dreams of giving his family a good life. He wants a nice house and a car, good education for his kids, to be able to travel the world, and a million more things. All these things require money, which he does not have.

In his study of the law of attraction, he learned that he has to be clear about what he wants. He could not decide which one he wanted the most so he made a list of the things that he wanted and why.

Joe's dream since childhood is to win the lottery jackpot just once, so he could turn his life around.

If he wins the lottery, he can have the house, the car, education and so much more. One by one, he scrapped each item until it boils down to just one thing, winning the lottery jackpot.

Now he knows what he wants to manifest.

- Dream. Do you still remember in the previous Chapter how visualization can help you? Doing visualization exercises will help you attract more positive vibes than negative ones. Bask in the feeling that your manifestation has happened.

Joe's story:

Joe's wife was a bit skeptical. She believed that their chance of winning the lottery is one in a million but her husband was determined.

He created a dream board. He put one dream board inside their bedroom and another in their kitchen. Joe wrote affirmations on post-it notes. He sticks them on their refrigerator and on the mirror in their bathroom.

Every morning when he brushes his teeth, he would recite his affirmations.

Joe started dreaming about what he would do with the money he won in the lottery. He tried to imagine it as if he already has the money.

He did this exercise every day without fail.

- Trust the Universe. It will deliver. Once you have set out your goal, you sit down and wait. Yes, wait. Trust the Universe that it will give you what you want. The Universe will give you signs that what you want is on its way, you just need to act on it.

  Joe's Story:

After several weeks of doing visualization exercises, Joe noticed that nothing seems to be happening.

The tickets he bought did not win him the jackpot. A couple of tickets won him a small amount but not his desired jackpot.

His wife started nagging him about his belief. She told him to give it up because nothing will happen. They will not get rich.

Joe ignored her at first but after a couple of more weeks, he too was ready to give up.

- Total belief and conviction. This is one of the main ingredients of a successful manifestation. If your belief and conviction are totals, you can wait without worry. You do not have to count the days to see how long you have been waiting. You do not question the Universe when will your desire manifest. The Universe will grant your desire when the time is right.

Joe's story:

One day his wife told Joe to just abandon the idea and let it go. Joe thought about this and told his wife that he will buy another ticket and if he still does not, he will abandon the whole thing.

Joe bought another ticket and waited. The draw came and Joe won another small amount, which is nothing compared to the jackpot amount.

Finally, Joe accepted that he would never win the lottery jackpot.

Joe felt frustrated and angry because he could not understand why nothing happened. He did everything right or did he? Did he miss doing something?

One day, Joe bumped into someone. He recognized the guy as the one who he met during one of that law of attraction coaching sessions he attended.

Joe was shocked to find out that the man is now a millionaire. He won in the lottery and not just once but twice since they last met.

Joe's first question was, how did he do it?

The man told him that he followed everything they learned in the session and it worked. Joe could not believe it because he did the same thing but never won.

Joe recounted everything he did but nothing worked. What did he do wrong?

The man smiled at him and told Joe that he too was frustrated after a few weeks and felt like abandoning the whole idea. The only thing that kept him going was his belief that it will happen and that he knows the higher power is working to get him what he wants most.

He continued to wait until it started manifesting. At first, it was little things. He started winning in raffle draws and then small wins in the lottery. He took this as a sign that the next draw will be his jackpot prize.

Joe was dumbfounded. He felt like all kinds of fool. It was there staring him in the face all along. The signs were there. They were given by the Universe but his belief wavered. He allowed his negative thoughts to rule him.

- Erase negativity. Doubts and fears are normal but do not let it rule your life. Do not deny negative thoughts but instead embrace them and then work your way around them.

Joe's story:

Joe went home feeling better. He knows what to do. He started doing visualization and affirmation exercises again but this time with a renewed determination and belief.

He did not tell his wife what he was doing so that her negativity will not affect him.

He went on with his daily life feeling happy and thankful. He started acting on signs that the Universe is giving him. There are times when he does not understand why he felt the urge to do something that is not part of his regular routine but he does them anyway. Sometimes, he gets surprised that when he does, something good comes out of it.

Then one day, on his way home he felt the urge to turn on the road opposite to his normal way. He did not question it but as he turned, he saw a lottery ticket stand recently opened. He was not planning to buy a ticket until the next day but he was already there and Joe thought it would save him time. Joe bought the ticket and went home.

Joe forgot about the ticket until after two days when his wife handed it to him. She found it in his pocket while doing the laundry.

Joe took the ticket and saw it has been drawn so he went to his computer to check online.

Joe almost had a heart attack when he saw the result. He won the jackpot prize and he is the only winner.

The icing on your cake

The law of attraction does not work like magic nor is it a robot that you can put on auto mode.

Just like baking a cake, you have to mix all the ingredients together. You place the mixed batter in the oven and you wait for a certain period until it is done.

The timing should just be right or your cake will either burn or flop.

To attain a successful manifestation, you need to mix the ingredients that would lead you towards your goal. You trust and wait that the Universe will grant your wish.

The law of attraction can change your life for the better, the manifestation success is just icing on the cake.

CONCLUSION

This book was not written to guarantee a lottery winning.

This book will help and guide you in increasing your chances to win the lottery by using the law of attraction.

Many things have been written about the law of attraction but in here, you will find some practical tips and techniques that many lottery winners used to manifest a lottery win.

The aim of this book is to help you strengthen your belief in the power of your mind and the principle of the law of attraction.

Success is possible if you want it.

You can achieve your dreams by believing in yourself and taking action to get what you want.

You cannot pass an exam if you do not study. No amount of thinking and believing can achieve that if you do not take action.

The same way that you cannot win the lottery, simply by wishing and believing you can win.

Ask yourself why you want to win. Is it because money will make you happy? Or is it because of the material things that money can bring you will make you happy?

It is not wrong to want money and an abundance of it. What is wrong is thinking the reason you need to have it is it can bring you ultimate happiness.

Ask any law of attraction coach and they will tell you the same thing.

The law of attraction will give the same vibration that you are sending out. A negative vibration will bring forth the same negative vibration and a positive one will attract the same positive vibration.

You can manifest your desire for money but do not let it be the sum and all end of your life.

If you want to make the law of attraction work for you, trust yourself to manifest what you truly desire and leave the Universe to deal with how you can get it.

THANK YOU!

Before you go, I just wanted to say thank you for purchasing my book.

You could have picked from dozens of other books on the same topic but you took a chance and chose this one.

So, a HUGE thanks to you for getting this book and for reading all the way to the end.

Now I wanted to ask you for a small favor. **Could you please take just a few minutes to leave a review for this book?**

This feedback will help me continue to write the type of books that will help you get the results you want. So if you enjoyed it, please let me know! (-:

www.ingramcontent.com/pod-product-compliance
Lightning Source LLC
Chambersburg PA
CBHW052102110526
44591CB00013B/2314